stoned words & electric flowers

Jerry Palmer
volume 1

Copyright © 2022 by Gerald Wayne Palmer I

All rights reserved. No part of this book may be used or reproduced in any manner whatsoever without written permission, except in the case of brief quotations embodied in critical articles and reviews.

ISBN 000-0-00000-000-0
First Printing 2022

Written, designed, and printed in Rankin County, Mississippi
and Grand Teton National Park, Wyoming
Cover uses Cooper Black and Cooper Nouveau typefaces
Body text uses Minion Pro typeface family
and the Cooper Nouveau typeface

All images appearing in this book are courtesy of
the Palmer Family Archives.

April 24, 1977
Dallas, Texas
Jerry Palmer
April, 2022

Paint Bucket Brigade Publishing
Rankin County, Mississippi

jerrypalmerauthor.com

Ruins

Looking at the streets, bridges, buildings, houses and barns.
All doomed to crumple in time, maybe tomorrow, maybe in a thousand years.
Either is but a tickle in the sands of time.
The grass and vines will cover the roads with the winds blowing the hail of silence.
Man was nowhere, for the earth has paid the price of having humans roam the plains.
As I looked on in awe it seemed real and powerful to try and reroute this fate.
Amounting to turning the hourglass over and over and over and over again.

January's Eyes

Nothing has changed since I sat at the top of the ridge.
On the far side of the mountain - words that haunt wandering thoughts.
Will the burning waters of shores still be touched?
Turn to mist with only the sight of torn hearts.
To sell diamonds is to rest on the white sands of liquid ghosts.
Useless are the words for soon they will be forgotten.

We must hold on to our lands not as sand but as rocks.
Are we closer to our dreams or have we tossed them all into the stream of time?

Sea of Wits

My thoughts are the same as others who have passed this unsure way before.
My will to continue must stay the fates of time itself.
I must have a gentle way in which to help others since many have come to my aid.
Sea of wits grant me an everlasting breeze even with the black of night; must I be a friend.
With butterflies floating between my thoughts walks a shadow of a lady.
Be at peace with this wanderer of my very soul.
She has to move across the meadows of memories which still burn.
Please turn the mist of time into clouds so it can rain a bit upon these coals so my words may rest.

It's the Journey

There is a search in everything I do and think of what I haven't found out.
Seems to be something I once had and like something I haven't yet touched.
Finding this treasure now would be too good.
Bound forever to carry out this search to the future.
P - is for the privilege of loving and being loved.
E - is for the ease it gives the mind and soul.
A - is for the absence in your search to find yourself.
C - is for the calm from liking what you find.
E - is for everlasting.
PEACE
    K C…1972

Hermit House

There is a room behind the log.
Here lives a fellow and his fun is in hiding here.
Yes - indeed he speaks in rhythm - this is the only way he came to keep time.
My - you say, but now it's a different way because of greed he lives in the log and spits into the fire - just to see if the flames will go higher.
Asking now to call him, sire.
Yes, we see because of taxes he has few lines to share.
But in closing he gladly leaves you a pair.
I learned to rhythm, charged only a dime.
But children beware, there is nothing really there.
In a box of riches, do you count every treasure and remember where it was found?
Or could you toss them aside and take this in stride?
Sometimes in worry more times in cheer,
I find myself looking for something so simple and yet being afraid to go near.

More Dirt

Takes more dirt to fill a hole than comes out of it.
Just goes to show that just because you have money,
doesn't mean you're rich.
And just because she's Witchy, doesn't mean she's not
kind and sometimes a bitch.
Pasted from you to me are things that make us high.
There are two places I wish to go.
1 - is the place you've never been,
2 - is the place you'll never go.

Looking Ahead

To see all that has happened.
To understand all sides is my burden.
It must unfold in another place rather than here.
For her thoughts are too close in my head.
Can't help to wonder if all's a circle forever spinning with no direction to turn.
All that seems clear is I must stay aware of my mind and what I feel is the right road.
Can't fall now for the journey has only begun,
it already has many different outlooks for what lies ahead.
Main thing is I must continue for if I stay here, I may well run into you.

Sad Lady with Fancy Matches

To be a wanderer of clouds is the fate you cast me upon.
Burning thoughts of your touch will follow until my spirit returns to the mountain range of time.
I saw you once as the sun turned to the west and the sky of tomorrow.
Fancy matches lit by a gentle river are seen by many

yet heard only by me.
She talked without me listening only to return to her home.
Your shoulders wear a proud cape - you walk toward a multi-colored glass.
Giving an image I can't see but the magic of mirrors can't stop the candle I burn for you.
The light by which I write struggles for the wax is gone only the wick burns in my lantern.
Its glow remains to flicker in the windows of the prison, surrounding the times when eyes met in a pasting oasis.
Stoned flames lit by fancy matches, sad-eyed lady longer, must I wait.
Couldn't talk to her so I write - pray the words will be read.
Before my memories turn to the wind then be lost in the sea of time.
Past this gate I must travel - to walk a path often used but soon to end.

Cronia

Out of the forest she came, upon her finger sat a bluebird.
At her feet rolled the mist of early morning.
Around her head flew a crown of butterflies colored in black and gold.
Wearing a dress of dew, she began to sing of the rising sun and weep for the leaving of the early day, where elves weave the dew upon the dress.
The moments I spent looking were filled with thoughts of you.
The birds sing where she once talked and the streams flow where she once walked.
At times when the world begins to spin slow - I gaze to a place
in time when nites were soft as silk, the day was bright as silver.
If as a circle it begins, as a circle it must end.
All I wish is that I had known ya…Cronia

September. 1975

Always

Wanted more than to receive your letters.
But used words and old poems is all I got.
In the spring the flowers are so sweet.
In the summer the smells are fresh.
In the fall the scent is gone.
In winter the flower dies, so has her love.
We met one day only to be lost the next.
We never touched just our lips.
Our minds traveled together as to the fair we went.
Now I can't see you, for you are afraid to be touched,
even for a moment.
Wondering and wishing you could travel near me,
this shall never be.
So alike are we, never will it be.
Yet each day will come again the sun will shine.
This love will never fade and the thoughts will never
change.
The wine we drank will remember the nights.
The smoke we saw will forever drift in my mind.
Only Your touch will ease the hurt left when the
fancy matches burned out.

Early Summer

Early summer is upon the sea flowing in my head.
Many days spent in the sun, riding a wheelbarrow.
Thinking of the things I should have done.
Learning is what I seek, old ways are what I'm fed.
A new place to think - a soft place to lay my head.
Some lady to turn my sadness into joy.
Yet in the end I'm always the toy.
Words are my product - tears are my comfort.
Black dresses dance in my brain.
Never knowing but wanting to remain the same.
This book is yet but a cry, to cry is to want love.
Love is all man has - none are they giving away.
The times are for the better, peace is only an effort away.
I know not what I want - I know what I have.
To this I give my blessings and to time I give my will.

Thirteen

Thirteen is the number of windows in my room.
Three doors, three belts, three shells and three men
of stone to guard my own.
Never to fade, for time is not part of the story I'm
beginning to read.
One person to live and not to hide your thoughts is
what you said.
Never be caged even if bars are your home.
Always longing for tomorrow with a train of words
in which to travel this world.
The pen will last, never will the ink fade.
Nor the sound of her voice begging for the love she
was refused.
Of a wicked ale I drink and of you I think.
Forgive this boy for he has only to dream of this girl.
Who came at the wrong time, stayed not for long.
Lessons have been learned and songs have been
forgotten.
Your cry for love will never be lost - always searching
no matter the cost.
For a lady who has something small of mine.

This Last Glass

The last time I loved it I cannot remember.
For it has been so long since that December.
Many miles have passed - yet tomorrow may bring another.
May the sunset always bring peace to your soul.
For joy is the food of our world, peace of mind be with us all.
May tomorrow bring the flowers of love to your heart.
May the stars light the path which you walk.
If you drift my way, sing a song of happiness.
Today will be spent in a joyful way.
May your tears be few - for I will cry them for you.
The heavens will unfold in your awakening.
The dove shall build her nest in your tree of life.
My love to you - I drink this last glass of wine.
…May 8,1974

Mississippi River

Played in your waters, laid upon your sandbars.
Looked under the bridges and fished upon your shores.
Still you roll along cursing man in a voice no one hears.
But the songs of the birds, the vision of trees in the waters
and the memories carried away will leave stains that will never go away.
From Cario to Orleans, what is the face of time but another bend or turn?
Fade with the sun, rise with the snow, no matter our progress, scars we leave.
Bones of the fish upon your banks, foam at your crest can't rest in our deltas.
For the levees are long and the valuable topsoil is all but gone.
Dumped my feelings into the river, as they floated away,
I couldn't help but shiver knowing it's so wrong to trash the river.
No use are they to me, for loose is my heart and my soul seems to have left me.
Don't feel bad, it's not the first love that went sour.
What I mean to say is ours was but an hour.
Didn't take hold yet will return in years to come.

Star Run

Rode thru the years as if they were meadows.
Looked to the sun, for answers when there were none.
Told our stories as if they would dry bitter tears and replace
the long gone years.
No more tracks and very few tears, cause we are of little matter.
Guess I ought to try and make this a little sadder.
Stars will be lost, stars will be found,
With your presence there is a sparkle which always will show, if it's the color of your eyes or the length of

your hair.
To those who read the above, read it again, a little slower and with a little more love.
November.13,1975

Called Once From the Road

Called her mom to get her number, on my way through town,
told her the heavens graced me with this love
I figured we had found,
which I carry with and in my heart .
She never understood what I meant long ago,
she drifted away as smoke will on a windy day.
As a special part of my heart decided to hide away.
For it wasn't hard to tell you had to say good-bye.
Friends never really part, so I wondered why you left in such a cheerful way.
I see now there were many things to gaze upon, with only a few words to say.
The saddest of all was to see her go and never know why it happened that way.
But thinking that all good things must go, yet wondering if they ever return?
Ice cream melts in the sun, the state fair always ends

just when you're having fun.
Ferris wheels don't look the same and probably never will.
Fires relit can burn hotter than before is what I came to learn.
Flames burn brightly, more so near the end.
Candles go quickly as we do my friend…

Woodstock

If you don't want my peaches,
don't shake my tree.
Pen and sword,
feather and stone.
Peaches and sugar,
wine and song.
Pass the time evenly
and find there's more to be seen
than is shown.

Crossvine

Smoke of the crossvine from the creek banks of Southern waters.
Where is fantasy bred?

In the heart or the head?
Guess not at the beginning do you wonder about your fate.
Walk as the wind blows everywhere just not in one place.
Wonder makes my wit, pasting makes the time.
Wonder how it will fit, pasting by wasting the time.
Expect - only to receive the gift you shall never leave.
A love you have wanted but never could hold,
needing to carry it gently knowing they broke the mold.
Can see now why I kept hanging on, couldn't really at the time,
nor could I see that what I wanted was already gone.

Hidden Creek

The search be the truth.
The search be the longin.
The search be the searcher.
Deep among the rivers, deeper among the souls.
Rolls the pairing and hearing of things told.
Ribbons of both color and light.
Here shines the sun, ever so bright.

White Light and Pure Emotion

Smell of Roses that never goes away,
Empress Josephine's castle smells of musk to this day.
Kathryn Susan will always bless my mind with the
scent of pure love, as finally known and worn like a
crown, days of flowers and weeks of longing, always
leads back to a memory.
Maybe a warning, who's to say,
a rose never wilts when
dried by the sun, always trying to redo what time has
done.

Lions rest while children pray,
children rest while Lions prey.
Eat the ice cream before it melts,
love her before she leaves
Ask for nothing - for there is nothing to save.
Nothing but the future and it started yesterday my friend.

While You're Away

You say I left you ashes - well you left me with tears.
Not for one nite but for a thousand years.
Meant to last forever but was destroyed the first day.
Our love now means nothing and there is no reason to stay.
Not because of the smiles but mainly because of the gifts.
You lay in wait ready to give someone the slip.
Careful of the footing so that you don't take a dip.
Find no place to rest, lookin for what you do best.
Who's to say, who will pay for living a life full of jest.
If you had your way and became queen for the day,
Would you change the world or leave it the same old way?
You have no choice but even if you did, the day would end and back to ashes you would spin.

Shell

Within so long, I don't know how to be without.
Laughed so long - till I could only shout.
Wrote the book and still don't know what it's about.
Built the roads and can't read a map.
Trimmed the trees but can't find the shade.
Prayed for a drink while I drowned looking at the

sink.
Left Jackson in a daze, found what I craze.
To walk like a man still feeling like a babe.
Peeled by the layers of doubt that roam freely in the thoughts.
Then block out the sun, filling my soul with dirt.
Here I'll plant the seeds hoping to grow my worth.

Sad But True

Sit here thinking whatever happened to you?
We took so many drives, found roadsides dark and lonely.
If we knew then what we know now - would change be made or just stay the same?
No difference to me does it make, for I found something time couldn't take.
Little to write, wondered what to say.
Didn't speak a word so she just walked away.
Perhaps in rythme I could reach her mind.
Wasn't to be, she fell for him not me.

Millsap Rock

Stone of sand - long will you stand,

thru rain and snow - long will your beauty show.
Perhaps the moon will crack and the sun will dry.
Never will you move in the life of I.
Flagstone flat, Millsap thick, Granbury rocks leaving only the bricks.
Heavy hobby gathering these stones making paths into tomorrow.
While Mexican kilns cooked soft sand bricks.

Half Star

But I loved her all the same.
All I remember was that we met and laughed .
Last time we met I cried, little does it matter about the rest, just in trying, we did our best.
As you walked to the door, I felt sure you would turn and ask for more.
This mistake I made, for now years have passed and for years I have paid.
Nothing will bring you back - nothing will return the time lost.
Knowing this I again would gladly pay the cost.
Of the stars in the sky, some you can see,
most remain out of sight, only knowing of their light.
Saw him die, saw her cry.
Makes you wonder if God takes a side, if not then why does she hide?
Perhaps the answer we shall never find.

Blue Dazes

Are all the loves painted in shades of blue?
Of all the girls I've met, none will be like you.
Saw this then and still it's true, for this reason all my loves have been blue.
That is unless someday I again happen upon you.
Too much to ask, too much to pay.
Seems as the blues will never go away.

Dog Days

Now in doubt, now in pain - can't do without can't make it rain.
Give you many, give you few - give you all - now what to do?
Gone but not lost, keep looking no matter the cost.
Your soul ain't free - gonna have to choose - just like me.
Win or lose, which will it be?
Past in time, fade in the sun - slowly look behind to see what's been done.
Past in time - write you a line.
No more to say, at least not today.

Age But A Number

Grace is by your side as you grow and your green eyes
continue to cast the spell.
Tell them, you're in love - with gifts from the stars above.
Pearls, diamonds and the silk purse, these you wore trying
to escape the treasures that haunt you like a curse.
Servant girls, bracelets and eyes that shine, clean and sparkle

all at the same time.
Age kissed the cheek and caressed the arm, no more are the parties to cheer the nite.
Now you sit and rock, glad for the day and thankful for your past.
Tho, I can't help but wonder if the diamonds turned to dust
and the stars began to rain,
Would you return to the same path or turn away early to avoid the tears.
Not what you wanted but it's what we got, now and forever
you can sit and rock.

Sad maybe the return, if we at first give in, not slowing always
continuing to run.
None does it matter for there is no one to care.
Climb the ladder - take it slow.
Cast no shadows, draw no stares, time itself gives all we can dare.

Hearing Bells

Bells of heaven may ring in your time.
You live for a light which you've seen fade away.
Of all the loves you had, only one remains.
Will you claim it now or when your ear is to the ground?

River Gypsy or Social Lite

Something lost, something gained.
Drink from the cup that sits before you - can't help but wonder about the girl, who makes the jars from the dust of stars.
Does she watch your life unfold?
For if she does, maybe she'll help you get a better hold.
It never hurts to be lent a hand, most of all when it'll help you make a better stand.

After Trying to Leave

Finding it wasn't much grief in leaving a misplaced belief.
Only in finding many people are strange, it's sad to say many will remain that way.
Think hard - is there really anyone to blame, if not themselves.
For they don't realize love is the game.
Wrongs or perhaps different songs need to be sung.
Holding back when wanting to run,
pushing when wishing to remain.
Not answering when asked,
yet asking when knowing there is no answer,
or at least one they're ready to hear.
It's why I pass you by, often it's the reason I sat with a stare...
Fewer are the these tears in the passing years, cause I've learned of your tricks from testing your fears.

Plant More Trees

Broke a mirror - stepped into the grass.
Made the mirror into a sun - took a little more grass and it was done.
Looking behind - looking to the side - looked in every place I could find.
No angle did I see - just you, Mother Nature and me.
Oh, what a pity - to live in the city.
Perhaps a garden or plant a tree - this got me by and Dirt Weed kept me high.
Decided to write ninety pages and never read the first.
Not anything special, just something for my thirst.
Plant a tree a day, water them well and then just walk away.
Words to be written, seeds to be sown.
What I am doing is something quite unknown.
June, 1977

Sister Years

Wrote this for yesterday or maybe the year before.
Had a wish that I gave her, it was to have you smile for a moment, and to ask for time to always keep you near.
So she keeps her smile - just as I was granted the wish many nights ago.
Often I feel a closeness telling me, you're near- as well the losing of your touch is all I fear.
As I have walked over the bridge of time.
Many are moments that weigh upon my mind.
Like planting a tree and later being able to sit in its shade.

Or putting a note in a bottle but never throwing it away.
Most are simple and most were right but of the ones left,
are the ones giving me fright.

Fly By

He flies into the night, looking for the brightest of lights.
Will he awaken from this with the sun?
Must be something about the city, gotta be the lights cause they're so pretty.
From dreams one can steal, no one else can feel.
She never knew what he said, all she knew was he kept a warm bed.
Now he's gone - what she did was wrong.
She's looking for a place to hide, finding this was not to be.
She lost the truth - now she stays high,
never saids much unless
you look her straight in the eye.
Cry for the one that waited, cry for the one that left,
weep for you speak with hate.
Pray for us all - that it's not too late.

Burning Angel

As a rabbit snared in a trap, so as he sat, wishing her back.
All his love and trust did she sap.
Now he carries his thoughts - written in a paperback.
Paid in silver for the lines he cried, not worth its weight in gold.
What's left of the heart she stole.
Pasting thru time, all he knows is he tried to love her.
Saddest for all tomorrows is the price she paid for breaking his soul.

Yes, my dear - her cost was a much heavier toll.
She indeed lost the goodness which was once her soul.

Tell Me a Story

Today is the day you walked away, now the sun is setting,
all I can do is watch the light fade.
After the lying I was bound to learn, cause so many times
you let me know.
Why people like us met, is a question to me, guess wine
(Boone's Farm) really does take a toll. Would you trade
time for gold and figures?
Is it just the price of being sold?
Run till you can't, don't know that's not the way.
Find another lover and may goodness be with you,
all along the way.

Stay

Just the idea of looking for her, then finding she was looking your way.
All that matters is something happens and having the right words to say.
Drink her wine, spend the time making the moments, hoping for her to stay.
After seeing her, loving her, missing her before she even leaves.
Your thoughts are of roses and perfume and black on black.
Robes and shoes, gowns and clues that it won't last.
Just feeling it's a nice shade of gray.
You cry your thoughts again for you didn't have anything to say.
That had not been said, even though a million sounds went through your head.

Petals of a Flower

Petals fall upon the ground, gone is your beauty which once made you proud.
Crumbled with grace, hiding in the silk and lace.
Given once and then taken away.
Youth has only one spring yet it lasts for years, now it's autumn and time as begun to show, telling you now there is much passion yet to show.
As a flower is picked it begins to fade ever so slowly and ever so sweet.
Your longing for love and your sweetness to me, count more than the weeds that grow near your feet.
A rose among briars is still a rose, but can't be reached no matter how hard I try.
Always and forever this has been shown, if more can be given, is it the soul I own?

High School Maidens

Who's Who was all in a dream, all the pictures would be of you.
Everyone would remember this year and you have nothing to fear.
One had a boyfriend, who was treated nicely but

dumped in the end.
From his happiness was he thrown for her cheating ways.
Lived in the shadows and Michael was never to know.
A witch by craft and a lady by trade, one of my best friends
but this I had to say.
Jo lasted longer than the glory she made, could run races
all over and still win the day.
All the boys cheered and the adults raved about the way
she played.
Little Bit did we know of the future and why we hid.
Once you hide and dare look inside things are different
and nothing is to my surprise.
Friend against friend
Brother against brother
Kinda seems like a war
But I guess that's what games we play are for.
November 6, 1975

Friendly Shadows

Remember the Indians - they lived in America
Remember the Birds - they flew in the Heavens

Remember the Trees - they gave birth in the soil
Remember yourself and how easy you were to spoil
May, 1976

First Year

Bracelet of silver. . .
Ring of stone. . .
in the rain I shiver
In the rain I'm cold.
When will I see your face?
When will you... I hold?
The years I knew you pasted as quickly

as snow on a spring day.
Few are my praises - for praises are dear
but one I'll give you - for that very first year
your heart was like frost
I loved you once - then I became lost.
Surely our gain was heaven's loss.
Jesters in a court never to be held
wanted to play the hand that never
was dealt - looked for this and nothing
else.
Life is a breeze - Take it with ease.
Sad thing is you never know when
the wind is gonna blow.

Ginny

Silk woven by a maiden's hand,
gold found by miners in a faraway land.
On the stage you wish to take a dance.
My eyes dear girl - tell me you have quite a chance.
The looks of a lady,
the heart of a baby.
Walking between the lines -
to sit in your swing beneath the vines,
talking of nothing - wishing for time.
Is something I once treasured
but due to your class - this wish
did not last. And for your thoughts
of me look to the past.

star lite
star bright
let her be - the first
star I see tonite

Sky Lake

Pass that of tomorrow - before this of today
lie all which I have seen. Either in true
sight or in sight of a dream.
Look to the woods - look to the trees.
Here lies the values of life and surely,

most are free.
Down the paths we walk - down
some we run. Across many bridges
through quiet fields. Out of the shade and into the sun,
if at all the stones you look
none will shine more - than the ones in the brook.
But be wise - look also into the skies
maybe you'll see something that'll
give you a surprise.
Yet Beware for the sun may
burn your eyes.

Twinkle

In search of the twinkle that lit the sky,
You have traveled far and found not a star.
For say - you might have missed this
treasure of light - passed it unknowingly
between day and night.
Among your dreams - this one you wear
as a ring. In all your days the course
has changed a little -
if you find this twinkle
will you hold it long -
or perhaps place it inside a temple?
Fold it neatly and stash it away.
Or wear it like a crown? Have the ladies woo you
and have the men frown.
Hurry now, for you mustn't be late
to find your silver-platter has become a paper-plate.
Please don't weep and surely don't cry
for just as you smiled - there was
A twinkle in your eye.

State Park

You may believe it's true,
then find that it's false.
You may love her madly
then turn to find her gone.
You may climb to the top
then find it's not a
long - drop.
If you do this - you may wish
to stop.
But only to look around and
view what you have found.
About yourself and the cards
You had to play…from the bottom to the top
isn't a long way.

Cut Flowers

Can't you see the writing
on the wall
...or don't you feel at all.
Babydoll made to cry - cracked her head
as she fell from the sky.
Lasted quite a while yet all that mattered
was that we remember her for a while.
Sunglasses she wore to cover red-eyes
made nice ash-trays.
Ivory toothpick which she gave to me
She also asked me to save.
To my wonder this charm did
I lose.
Now in the shade-trying to fade cause
I found little to save.

Becky

When she walks - it's in a fancy little way.
Becky talks very Southern - yet in
her sassy little sway. Blonde and cute, with eyes
which shoot.
She'll tell you she's lonely and perhaps
She is.

Shirley Pickens

Cute as the morning light -
cast a spell with her fairy tales.
love you for your words -
yet when we speak - are we heard?
She'll make you think of Shirley Temple
sharp to the eye - quick as a whip.
Take her gently for she's a gentle maid.
All the things you may give her will
never amount to what I gave.
This I gave her and she promised
her love to save.
But I see now
her words are as empty
As the spot I save.

Blue Bottles

Remains in a Bottle
dust upon the shelf
Now she saves you - when
She has nothing else.
Casting shadows upon the wall
She plays with figures as
They grasp her attention.

You've taught her little
or little has she learned
that will please her when
the fires die and the ashes settle
the frost has been sown
where will she lay
if not in a bed of hay.

A moment has gone and
A window left open.
Soft words are spoken
And repeated in time.
Now she is awake
But the dust upon
The shelf is gone…

Drawings upon a bottle -
Catch your eye. The figure
is not clear - for in what

I saw caused a tear to fall
it was not the figure
that made me cry
tis was the dust and where
I had seen it last.

Speck of dust
Could be us
But all these words
And not no Trust.

Sunset Walker

Perhaps she's not much
of a talker -
Riding the time
All for the sliver -
Perhaps she'll want gold.
After the sun-sets everything is cold.
You've felt my heart-caught my eye
held me softly - waved good-bye.
If tonite you
walk in the Rain -
Do you wonder why,
So many things aren't explained -
Hands on a clock,
The wind and the rain,
Pieces of a puzzle,

our lives are much the same.
Is it not so bittersweet
That angels should walk the street?
Darkest Star, darling you are.

Peacock

Many things have passed - can I be
sure that tomorrow won't be like
the day before? Crazy are these dreams
and still may they come true? Closer
seems the ease that is sought. On
blows the wind - and with it she came.
Last nite in a place filled with colors

Colors of many shades
Sounds of many voices - all crying out.
Can you hear me or do you
wish to listen? My words are of
no meaning until they are heard -
Or may we travel together and be
miles apart. I am not a stone - in
the passing suns I shall crumble but
the pieces shall spread with the water -
Look back with joy - for good times
were many - Think of the words
I have written - all of which
Are sent to you.

Two Birds

My days seem to past with a
gentle push from a slow wind.
Time passes not the same for all - but for
the many that try to stand in her
path. A mind full of something
with the path not fully shown.
Silkworms bury my sorrows
in a web as glamorous as the
cloth of a distance lady - who
ponders in a cycle never ending.
I couldn't talk to her so I shall
write and pray the words will be read -
before my memories turn to the
wind - and be lost in the sea
of time.
Past this gate I must travel - to
walk a path often used -
but never to end. Only to spin.

Pasture Flowers

In the silence there lies
a laughter that only the sad
can hear.
In the darkness there lies

a sparkle that only the lost
can see.
And in the confusion of
the pieces that are left of me
there lies a teardrop meant
for you - Carobeth
For in my silence there isn't much
I can hide. Even if I desired
there's not much that's left inside.
Yet if there's anything left to show
let it be shown - for I too would
like to know.
Raw mushrooms from where the thistle grows.

Wonize

Drew you a pitcher -
in which to pour time.
Now if you find opening - do not
leave it behind

Sugar-spoons
and the girl that saves them.
She knows they always shine
it's just that the tarnish
wears a heavy coat.

Now at it you look
not really a book
just only a passing
no more than a look.

Meaning to buy nothing - yet
paid for it all.
Free the bird to the trees
in the woods.
Fly until tomorrow
and we shall see.
For you - who are wanting.
What will the answer be?

1 Way-Street

Funny to watch people frown -
most of all in your hometown.
Guess that it's the saddest in
their eyes - cause if it was
me - that would make it easy
to see.
Once went to the First church
wasn't long before we felt the hurt -
The Book said to forgive and to share -
Leon asked to be married.
But there wasn't love to spare -
Preacher said the wedding was not
to be held there.
I wasn't told until much later
was it better
Or was it worse?
Never really care
for I saw there was nothing to share.

Crazy Times

Cries of a madman fill the nite,
four years has he wondered.
Four years full of fright…
noble of death - doomed by a wretch

late one nite…
She burned his writing and cursed his name,
all she wanted was to save his soul.
She felt what he had written was not to
be told.

Jenny

Now thru the nite she walks alone
No one to touch her - no one to hold
She lives by herself and knows
no one else.
Worshiped the winters,
why - because of the wind

and the feeling she gets as she
walks through the cold.
Her name was Jenny
that's all you need to know.
Besides she died without a penny
As she sat lazy in the snow.
Lies of a sadman full of fright.
Dreams of an angel as she took flight.

Toy Surprise (Inside)

Living a life of a crackerjack box,
hoping that somewhere inside…
you'll find a prize.
If you find a small book - don't
throw it away - better read it - could have
something to say.
Paper inside a cookie, tales of your fate.
Read it again or perhaps just wait.
You're lucky if you find a penny
for say you find a nickel.
This may mean you're very fickel.
Or it may say if you find
a feather - use it in the right way
You may get a tickle.

Glass Dolls

Sit upon the shelf -
She acts as if there is nothing left.
Brass bells - seashells,
crystal balls and that ain't all.
She put all the things up
that would fall.
But I saw something in the hall -
I swear it was an angel
with silver-wings -
sort-of like one in
my dreams.
Any way I have been known
to see stranger things.

She wore a gown of smoke
that seemed to swirl around her
like a gray rope.
One more look is all I hope
for without this angel,
there is much danger - more I won't say.
For all of you know the way.

The Last Bird Flies Alone

...

Appleman

Appleman - whatever you wish it's yours
to have. You can sing all you wish
yet don't sing too loud.
Seeing a picture is lost on words.
Knowing all it said is always heard.
Hearing that tomorrow - is just a hill.
Pass today for something with a little
more feel.
If we listened to

all that was said -
Down which path do you
think we would be led?
If in a hurry we live
will in a hurry we die.

Tell Me a Lie

Tell me dear girl..
Touch in the arm
go very gently -
you're very far
from harm.

Time And Time Again

Nite before all was fine - till you found
you're not the only one in line.
Just thinking of what you told
me many days ago - that no matter
how I cried - you were forever to
be by my side.

Games of the mind.
Games of the soul.
Tell me dear one…
what secrets do
you hold?

Ashes to ashes.
Dust to Dust.

Words to words.
So as my trust,
did you sweep away
as if it were dust.

The eyes of a child can see…
the world spinning round.
All the music seems - but only
a sound. You're sure of your
being - but not quite sure
of your seeing.

Sat by a stream and watched it freeze
as the ice formed and made a crust.
You could see the future and those
you could trust.
I laughed at the ice - telling it - that
I thought it was very nice but I
wish not to see the future yet
if I do it will be in real life.

As the ice began to melt
it tried to tell me something else -
That tomorrow will go as surely as
it came and to look around - for none is the same…

Wandering... Wandering

In this world of folly and play - have you
ever noticed how it's the good things
That always slip away?
Of the children that dance or the ladies that sway
there are but few who play all day.
Back to the day - it's a strange word
That's the least you can say -
Many things happen once and
They happen everyday.
if not for the nite - we
would be lost in a day.
He told his story
And the words were not heard.
Well not the same way
As he meant to say.
So now he walks in quiet
seeing that in silence
is the only way.

Little Bit

Pieced together like a vase
told I was hopeless - totally a waste.
No heart do I have or maybe it's
a vapor of gas.
For a heart do I search but knowing my
journey is a picture book at last -
for my true heart did lie with
the past.
Just as a Kite thrown to the wind
high I did Rise then began to spin.
Guess I'll never know what it all meant
number 10

quarter-mile took her little time
I took her a little ways -
Tho I often wonder how she now spends
her days - the colors she likes and the flowers she craves.

Flower Child

Flower child - why did you go?
you were so close to what
you know was wanted.
When we started the world was full

of people hating each other - for reasons
Known to the minds of evil.
You were the blessed children of
a mistress unknown. Just a gentle
breeze in the burning minds of man.
Your music is quiet as we make
our way down the misty lane. But
when the staircase is unveiled - You
my princess will have your throne
And Rise above all heights we
have known.

Hippie Died 1968
Freak Born 1971
Flower child lives forever

Black Heart

Into a garden I walked
to the daisies I talked.
One spoke my name - I've heard her voice before
the tone was the same as when she walked
out the door.
Another spoke her words as if they were
a stream - carried me away as I fell into
a dream.
As I awoke - there before me was
the raging sea full of life

Everyone trying to swim upstream
makes things a-bit uneasy.
Is it so hard to float?
it's a much smoother ride in a boat.
Just as the bitter wind is better
with a coat.

Cry Me A Tear

Tears in her eyes, chill in her bones
hole in her pocket, hole in her soul
she lays in the way of what can be

a terrible waste.
Cause she wanted so much but took
it in quite a haste…crying is a waste.

Dead Flowers

Place them between the pages and gently
close the book -
Roses to last forever - caring always
to take another look.
Wax-paper saves her love - a candle in
the window saves a spice of a world
gone cold.
Never sees the sun but far from harm.
She's too busy having fun - got
something to do with having
to Run and Run and Run.

Stems and Petals

For a child of tomorrow to be living
today. These times of wonder ARE
passing for a second time -
To see words and know their
meaning

To see words and if they rhyme.
Put them together - just to past
the Time.
A laugh and a purr
told who you were
Playing of cards tell little
of skill and amount of luck.
All that in passing is the
making a buck.
Writing songs saying who's wrong
can't blame them - surely can't blame HIM
Once you held the flowers.
Now you hold only the stems.

Both-Ways

Cast unto the wind -
Thrown into the sea.
No more are the coins -
for I take the last with me.
Waves may wash the pennies -
but in your hands
there will never be gold.
Play both ways and you'll know
it's no fun. But it might be
a-little if you happen TO HAVE WON.
No matter the sprain
No matter the pain

No matter what friends
say.
Yet there's no way for me to say -
how much fun it is going one-on-one.

More Words

Stand here a moment - hold it dearly,
look very close and you can see
it clearly.
It's only a crystal that formed in the haze
made a picture that no-one can save.

Blow it off - and maybe it'll return.
But surely as it does - your walk
will become a run.
And there will be no way to
return from where you began.
I say this for a purpose
meant only for a few.
Read it again and you may
find it was for you...

Grapes

A high of gods in egos past -
That can see the shore as the
Sun shines -
A ship began a trip at quarter-mast
Now it lies in a CAVERN that
is always dim.
My thought to you
is never pour past the rim.

Green Eyes

Her eyes are like the silent spring
snow forever is the stare - but only

the breeze is left - to blow the flakes.
And the birds left to sing
And fly freely in the air…Love of
unspeakable passion just laid by and enjoyed the
action.

Willard

I met you at a time of sorrow -
You turned this to joy.
I loved you with my mind -
You turned this into a toy.
I met you with a closed thought -
you gave me a sea of reasoning.
I loved you till you had my all -
you gave me a sense that I will
TREASURE forever. Forever may be
short so forget me not and
perhaps if there had been another
Day - things might have been another
way.

Naughty

Of all the dolls and stars
I wonder how you made it
this far?
last time you walked away you winked
and said "Enjoy this day for never again
Will you see me this way?"
You're just a joke trying to show someone
that you're not just plain folk.
Talk all the way with your drink in hand.
No - you're not funny.
IS there one who'll take your money?
Yes - dear I'll call you honey - take you
to the coast and stay on the beach
Ready to make a TOAST. There's no more
use - not after you gave so much abuse.
Besides your glass is empty and there's not
Any more juice…

Again

Don't ask what I thought, for if you see this there is no need
to think.
I just knelt in the water and had a drink.
Sugar to the taste but what a waste, to serve this in a cup.
Instead of a book for all to view and all to look.
Took a glass full home and sat it upon a shelf.
There it remained for my friends to see.
None dared taste but all treasured a look.
So please won't someone help me publish my book.
For a penny or a dime, it doesn't really matter
you still get a look every time.

Verse

Seeing things a bit clearer as I go along,
sometimes I, catch myself listening to a verse
and thinking it's the whole song.

Without You

Look for the rings that were lost in the water.
Such a small thing falling into the stream.
Sort of like a dream, find a pond with the bottom
all covered with ice.
Tasting the water, finding a taste of spice.
Break each other's hearts, cause each other pain.
Without thinking anymore then having to explain,
all that really mattered seems to have been the
dream.
With the last ring falling into the stream.

Please Look Away

We pray this will last yet it seems we pray to the past.
Pray for the things you never had, this is why I look
and turn away so sad.
Go to the sky, make a wish then tell me of your
journey.
I'll tell you which is which, be she a woman or be she
a witch?
Just a tease that came with the breeze, just a girl
I loved with ease.

Just Thinking

A thought in thinking turns to a memory.
Remembering makes an idea.
Considering it becomes something I forgot.
The writing may fade from you but I will not.

Southerner

Your shining grace has begun to rust
The cloud with a lining has turned to dust.
The glass that you drank from -
has been broken.
All your words of worry
have been spoken.
At first there was hope of a tale
of glory - now you see that it
was the same old story.
Might have been better if you had
a little trust - but now I remember
that was one of the first
things to rust.
Thirteen rose and thirteen fell, all slave owners burn
in hell.
The states of the South rose to question the power
and were crushed by its might.
Yet we all travel in the shadows of wrongs done,
can we ever make them right?

Remember
the Jackson State Killings
- 1970

Back of a Mirror

did I know you for real
or just that moment when
our world was quiet and if
we wanted a high -
you didn't have to Buy it.

Grenada Dazes

Swam within my soul as the
betta swims in his bowl.
I became mastered by my senses.
I comfort my touch with her.
My taste with wine,
my hearing with the music,
my sight with the mountains.
My nose lingered
to the smell of roses.

My memory hears a wingsong
time passes a-long.
At the top of the water the betta
rests.
At the top of time I rest - try to see my view.
Woodstock…
For most everyday

I think of you.

No Reason

Sitting with no reason to stand.
Knowing how to behave - no reason to rage.
Caught loving the time - no reason to
look behind.
No reason had I for loving you -

if in times ahead you look backwards,
and wish to be there instead.
Surely beware for the darkness of the past
may put you there.
You may never know and never really care.
No reason to write except
to put a light burning at nite.
No reason to die except to
return to the sky.
All in a day,
did it go away,
and there's nothing
left to say.

Tales of the flame
only leave smoke -
and talk of a man
and what he did claim.
To leave…

In memory of -
Tommy
Steve
Dennis
Ronnie
Michael

Little Bit to You

In a box of riches
do you count every treasure
and remember where it was found?
Or could you toss them a side
and take this in stride?
One or both mustn't be a hard ride.
Sometimes in worry
more times in cheer -
I find myself looking for something
so simple and yet so afraid to go near.
A Box
with 4 sides and only 1 top
Turned it over and the top became the side
a side
to stand by and a place to be
and certainly out of the way
A way to be - from me…

Silent Walk In The Waves

She wore a gown of morning flowers,
waves of the sea were quiet as she walked along the beach.
Nobody knows and she thinks nobody cares but she kept looking for something to be found in the

pasting of the year.
Shadows on the wall - show your presence but what will show your departure and your disappointment?
If not, my tears, surely living for another year.
From walking slowly, ya can get a better view.
This we have seen yet our numbers are few.
In all I have learned there's only one matter
in which I have concern,
It's to look at the children and watch them smile,
pray that they are strong, for this walk may take a while.
Upon the stage all seems to rage, who's looking from behind
the curtain.

Perhaps it's the wealthy, wishing to play but with nothing to say.
People are crying for answers and still nothing is done.
Shall we gather in the streets or wait, ride the time until goodness has defeated the hate.
This is not happening and soon it may be too late.

Lost Time Never to Return

…did you tell them in time perhaps you would meet again?
Did you tell her that she lives forever in your memories
and you were but a grain of sand?
You wouldn't see me -so I turned away - up I ran -up I ran.
I feel as if one reaches yet I see no hand.
In a box I kept my fears - to protect myself from time,
laughter and the jeers.
If by my side you stand, take it in stride, hope you are brave
for perhaps you, time will save.
Only then will you make a bid… just hide your love when you open the lid.
I broke more than I could ever mend.
Yes, I'm sorry but it doesn't help when you lose a friend.
If you are listening - please hold judgment till the end.
January 15, 1976

Wait Don't Go

He waits at the station, standing in the rain.
You can believe there's something about you,
he can't explain.
Could be your thoughts or the perfume, maybe
the rings you wear.
Noticing the flowers in your room as he wants to
leave,
knowing it's too late.

He comes to the fact this is as long as he dares wait.
Weigh broke the bridge and across the bridge
again he must cross.
Or it maybe the treasure you keep in your heart,
swearing no one would have it,
from this treasure of trust you would never part.
Well for a time you kept your heart safe.
From you, he said "he would never part".
But today turns to tomorrow and tomorrow turns to yesterday.
He turns to you and you turn away.
What's left no one can say, but for the start you should never
let the trust go as it was held in your heart,
now of which he is very much a part.
December 11,1975

Kiss a Sister

Tell her your fear - may she love you dearly and
help you see more clearly.
Blow wind, blow her near, bring her gently and in
good cheer.
If there ever was a moment I cherish , it happened
when you were close at hand.
Now my summers are chilled, my winters are harsh,
the springs are the saddest and during the falls I
venture near maddness.

Light from her eyes is a gaze caused by others missing and with hurting tries.
One left her crying, the other chilled her by lying.
Now I am caring for her, finding her very strikingly similar
to a lightning bolt before the thunder
I wonder at this girl of love, does she have plenty or does she have any?

Old Stories

Lying to myself, finding not a truth.
Turned my head, saying what's the use.
All to be found was once lost before.
Kinda makes living a bit of a chore. Walking the miles,
touching the branches,
seeing not a tree. Hoping to find some light
before more darkness finds me.
Feeling only pain, wiping it away as if it were rain.
Wondering at all things which were never explained.
She's never worth the trouble, always wanting her to stay.
But when she does, I wonder why things are this way.
Knowing better but wanting more than I can stand,
never claimed to be smart just yearning to be her man.
When she stays, what becomes of the next day,

beauty in front of the mirror.
Me standing in the hall, all for the beauty of this hour
and the way she makes me want to crawl.
Steel guitars and mason jars makes it easier to see,
that all the truth holds is; You are you and I am me,
all the rest we'll just have to wait and see.

Short Burst of Fire

Shorter the candle higher the flame
must be why you're to be remembered not only for
your name.
Flowers will be sent after being cut from the stalk,
placing it in a vase after which all will be tossed.
Wine will be drank, songs will be sung for
the memories of the old, and the hopes of the young.
Roses are sweet to smell, birds are sweet to hear,
Kathy, you are too sweet to me and I'm afraid
you'll disappear.
Glitter could spell your name or it be chiseled in
stone,
No better sound than that whisper in my ear.
Water pours from the sky yet never again will I cry.
My case I rest, head upon your chest.
Wishing for you the best and that I may always ride
this wave at its crest.

Walking Down the Flower Lane

Walked hand in hand, touch and a squeeze.
Touching at the hips and rubbing at the knees.
Kicking the hours as if there was no end.
Climbing up towers only to rest and start again.
Left her only for a moment, but only a moment did it take
for her to lose the way.
Never will I find her in these woods, knowing this would be the journey away from the path we took..
The note she left said she was extremely busy and I must go.
Free your world of hate before you look around,
Realizing it's probably already too late.

As I Go

A candle I will light, to give something to the darkness of nite.
Stare into the dark, thinking of nothing only to be alone.
Not hard as it seems - first you lose your heart, happiness and all the dreams.
Getting rid of the baggage to lighten the load.

Then all is gone and you're the only one in town sitting
at the square, wondering why any of this has value.
If sadness is the way, be sad for those who have nothing,
because you threw all yours away.
Little does it matter but great does it seem.
All we had together has tumbled through life
as this wonderful dream.

Waiting For You

Looking at the sky, telling myself that time isn't really crawling by.
Not to worry, surely best to get high.
It really is a lot of fun - thinking of things to do, waiting for you.
Like a flower set back by the frost, are you always late or did you get lost?
A lot of fun writing lines, alot of fun twisting rhymes.
But looking for you is where I send most of my time.
Once I lived in a treehouse, it wasn't much but I was off the ground.
No matter where they looked I was nowhere to be found.
Crossed the waters only to find land on the other side.
Isn't easy to forget but it's not easy to remember.
The last days and the way they were spent.
It's like you were heaven sent, gave me spice.
Touched my life again, now that makes twice.
Laughed till winter, walked in flowers then back to heaven you went.

Little Trees

Tell me of your broken branches and of the lost leaves.
Run over by mowers, cut by saws and stolen by thieves.
Planted in the pot, with holes in the bottom
so the roots don't rot.
Travel with him as a friend and confidant, hiding the hurt.
Of a crazy road lizard which crossed our path more than once.
Little trees grow strong from the winds and soon are grown.

Back Over Your Shoulder

Turn to look around, tell me what you found,
in your dancing thru town.
If it be glass or if it be diamonds, tuck them away
to make them of value another day.
In finding twigs leave them where they fall, perhaps a robin
may use them to build her nest.
No matter what is found you have no choice
but to look around.

Need the Moon

This girl loved the land, even planted roses
and seeds with her hands.
Now she sleeps because the sun is high in the sky.
Its rays of light are good for all,as the moon is needed
by the maiden.
Once she played in the meadows and waded in the
river, time now will tell if she cries in vain or can the
levee hold back the rain.

Sad Truth

Sad but it's true, I got everything just by loving you.
They say it never shows yet there it is in plain sight.
But I can tell just by saying your name.
So bear with me as I try to make you laugh, my words often seem sad.
If I can help you smile and rest for a while, my task is finished.
All that remains now is for the freedom of looking for a treasure to find..I'll have to leave the past behind.
Turn to tomorrow, learn from my sorrow.
Find my last love, so I'll look for the time given,

hoping with prayer that the green-eyed goddess is still there.
January 19, 1976

State Of Mine

Once it looked as if the world might be able to live together
but now I wonder.
People must realize only they can make this a world of peace.
We seem doomed for the whole system is about to crumble.
It might be better - it is time for a change.
I guess in time we will know if we made it.
Seems all so simple for man to stop fighting wars and try to live as one.
We have seen killing is not the way and man is strange,
you can't say what will happen next.
If they slow down and become aware there isn't much time left.
Strange is the way of my mind, knowing the way things should be.
Yet time is the only key which unlocked the vast wonders
before me.

It seems truth will be put forth in a way just out of our reach.

Looking around, seeing signs of no matter what I think or do,
it has been done in the past.
This being true, why must things be as they are?
With just a little help from each of us, perhaps
we will make it through.

Empty Space

As we enter the last years of the 20th century
one can only wonder and dream of our life in the
early years of the 21st century.
We have seen on tv, many of the tools/toys
we will be able to use. All these - just to keep
from singing the blues.
Yet there never has been less of a chance of war
between now and then. If there's to be no war,
man must surely look beyond the limits of his
own nation and try to understand his brother
no matter his creed.
Not to be a statesman and not to be a writer of events
comes hard - yet I am wise enough and
I can take its hints.
Wanted to be wrapped in glory and have something
to tell but the song had been sung and

that ruined the story.
Knowing that fear is only a thought which lies forever near.
What has been done wrong cannot be changed, so with the right will remain the same.
If I had started it years before, I wonder what would have been in store.

Write a Will

To give you this and to give you that.
Give them my rocks to build a road.
Give them my words so they can sing a song.
Give her my picture so she won't be alone.
Give her my stash so she can get stoned...

The End